How to Start Your Own Business

A Guide For Beginners 2024

Iryna Veskera

Copyright © 2024 Iryna Veskera

All rights reserved.

DEDICATION

Dedicated to all the fearless business starters who dare to dream, innovate, and shape the future.

CONTENTS

	Introduction	i
1	Chapter	1
2	Chapter	Pg 5
3	Chapter	Pg 9
4	Chapter	Pg 12
5	Chapter	Pg 17
6	Chapter	Pg 23
7	Chapter	Pg 29
8	Chapter	Pg 35
9	Chapter	Pg 41
10	Chapter	Pg 47
	Conclusion	Pg 53

INTRODUCTION

Starting your own business is an exciting and transformative journey, but it can also be overwhelming and fraught with challenges. This book, "How to Start Your Own Business - A Guide For Beginners," is designed to be your companion on this journey, providing you with the knowledge, tools, and inspiration you need to turn your entrepreneurial dreams into reality.

In today's dynamic and fast-paced world, more people are choosing the path of entrepreneurship. Whether driven by a desire for independence, the pursuit of passion, or the need to innovate, starting a business has become an attractive option for many. However, the path to success is not always clear, especially for those new to the world of business. This book aims to demystify the process, breaking down complex concepts into manageable steps. It is crafted specifically for beginners who may feel overwhelmed by the abundance of information and the myriad of decisions that need to be made.

By the end of this book, you will have a solid understanding of the essential elements required to start and run a successful business. You'll learn how to generate and validate business ideas, develop a robust business plan, navigate legal requirements, secure financing, build your brand, and manage daily operations. Most importantly, you'll gain the confidence to take bold steps forward, knowing you have a comprehensive guide to support you every step of the way.

This book is for anyone with a budding interest in entrepreneurship. Whether you're a recent graduate eager to carve out your own path, a professional seeking to break free from the 9-to-5 grind, or a stay-at-home parent looking to turn a hobby into a profitable venture, this guide is tailored to meet your needs. It's also an invaluable resource for those who have already taken the first steps in their entrepreneurial journey but need guidance to navigate the complexities of starting and sustaining a business.

Understanding that starting a business can be intimidating, this book addresses common concerns such as fear of failure, lack of experience, and uncertainty about where to begin. Each chapter is designed to build your knowledge incrementally, providing practical advice, real-life examples, and actionable steps. From finding the right business idea to scaling up operations, this book tackles the challenges head-on, offering solutions and insights that are easy to understand and implement.

Join us on this journey, and let "How to Start Your Own Business - A Guide For Beginners" be the catalyst that turns your entrepreneurial aspirations into reality. With the right guidance, resources, and mindset, you can create a business that not only survives but thrives in today's competitive landscape.

1 UNDERSTANDING ENTREPRENEURSHIP

Starting your own business is like embarking on a thrilling adventure—full of potential, challenges, and opportunities. Before you dive in, it's crucial to understand the essence of entrepreneurship. This chapter will lay the foundation by exploring what entrepreneurship truly means and the mindset required to succeed.

What is Entrepreneurship?

At its core, entrepreneurship is the process of creating, launching, and running a new business. It involves identifying a market need, developing a product or service to meet that need, and assuming the risks and rewards associated with the venture. Entrepreneurs are often seen as innovators, bringing fresh ideas and solutions to the market, and driving economic growth through their ventures.

The key concepts of entrepreneurship include innovation, risk-taking, and value creation. Innovation is the lifeblood of entrepreneurship, whether it's a groundbreaking new product, a novel service, or a more efficient way of doing something. Risk-taking is inherent in the entrepreneurial journey, as starting a business involves uncertainty and the potential for failure. However, it is through taking these calculated risks that entrepreneurs can achieve significant rewards. Finally, value creation is the ultimate goal—delivering something of value to customers, which in turn generates value for the entrepreneur and stakeholders.

The Entrepreneurial Mindset

While understanding the technical aspects of entrepreneurship is important, cultivating the right mindset is equally crucial. The entrepreneurial mindset is characterized by several key traits and attitudes that enable entrepreneurs to navigate the ups and downs of their journey.

Successful entrepreneurs are driven by a clear vision of what they want to achieve and a deep passion for their idea. This vision acts as a guiding star, helping them stay focused and motivated, even when faced with obstacles.

The road to entrepreneurial success is often fraught with setbacks and failures. Resilience—the ability to bounce back from challenges—and perseverance—sticking with the journey despite difficulties—are essential traits for overcoming hurdles and continuing forward.

The business landscape is constantly changing, and entrepreneurs must be able to adapt to new circumstances, pivoting their strategies when necessary. Flexibility allows entrepreneurs to respond to market shifts, customer feedback, and other dynamic factors.

Entrepreneurs must think creatively to identify unique opportunities and solve problems in innovative ways. This creative thinking often leads to the development of products and services that stand out in the market.

While risk-taking is a fundamental part of entrepreneurship, successful entrepreneurs manage risks carefully. They conduct thorough research, plan meticulously, and make informed decisions to minimize potential downsides.

Entrepreneurs often work independently, requiring a high level of self-motivation and discipline. Setting goals, maintaining focus, and managing time effectively are critical for driving progress and achieving success.

The entrepreneurial journey is a continuous learning process. Entrepreneurs must be open to acquiring new skills, seeking feedback, and learning from their experiences, both positive and negative.

Understanding and embracing the entrepreneurial mindset sets the stage for success. It's about more than just starting a business—it's about adopting a way of thinking that prepares you for the challenges and opportunities ahead. As you move forward in this book, keep these principles in mind. They will not only help you in the initial stages but will also serve as a compass throughout your entrepreneurial journey.

Benefits and Challenges

Entrepreneurship offers a unique blend of benefits and challenges. Understanding both can help you prepare for what lies ahead and make informed decisions.

Why People Start Businesses

Many people are drawn to entrepreneurship for the freedom and independence it offers. The ability to be your own boss and set your own schedule is a powerful motivator. Additionally, the potential for financial rewards can be significant, especially if your business idea is successful and scalable.

Passion also plays a crucial role. Many entrepreneurs start businesses based on their interests or hobbies, turning what they love into a profitable venture. This passion often fuels their perseverance and dedication, helping them push through tough times.

Moreover, the desire to solve problems and make a difference in the world drives many to start their own businesses. Entrepreneurs often seek to address unmet needs or improve existing solutions, contributing positively to society and the economy.

Common Challenges and How to Overcome Them

Starting a business is not without its hurdles. One of the most common challenges is securing adequate funding. Many entrepreneurs struggle to find the capital needed to launch and sustain their business. Overcoming this involves thorough financial planning, exploring various funding options, and sometimes starting small and scaling up gradually.

Another significant challenge is the fear of failure. The uncertainty inherent in starting a new venture can be daunting. Developing a resilient mindset, setting realistic goals, and learning from failures can help mitigate this fear. Embracing failure as a learning opportunity rather than a setback is crucial for long-term success.

Time management is also a critical issue. Entrepreneurs often juggle multiple roles and responsibilities, leading to burnout. Effective time management strategies, such as prioritizing tasks, delegating when possible, and maintaining a work-life balance, are essential for sustainable success.

Market competition presents another challenge. To stand out, entrepreneurs must thoroughly understand their market, identify their unique selling proposition, and continuously innovate. Staying adaptable and responsive to market trends can help businesses maintain a competitive edge.

Lastly, maintaining a steady cash flow can be challenging, especially in the early stages. Proper financial management, including regular cash flow analysis and maintaining a buffer for unexpected expenses, is vital. Building strong relationships with suppliers and customers can also contribute to more predictable cash flow.

Recognizing these challenges and preparing to address them proactively will equip you with the resilience and strategies needed to navigate the entrepreneurial landscape successfully.

Types of Businesses

Choosing the right business model is a pivotal decision for any aspiring entrepreneur. This choice will influence your legal responsibilities, tax obligations, and personal liability. Understanding the different types of business structures can help you make an informed decision that aligns with your goals.

A sole proprietorship is the most straightforward and commonly adopted form of business ownership. It is an unincorporated business owned and operated by one individual. This model offers simplicity and ease of setup and management, requiring minimal legal paperwork. The owner retains complete control over all business decisions, and profits are taxed as personal income, which can be advantageous. However, the owner is personally liable for all business debts and obligations, putting personal assets at risk. Additionally, raising capital is usually limited to personal savings and loans, and the business's continuity is tied to the owner's presence, potentially ceasing if the owner retires or passes away.

A partnership involves two or more individuals who share the profits and losses of a business. This structure allows for shared responsibility and the pooling of skills, knowledge, and financial resources. Profits are passed through to partners and taxed as personal income, which can be beneficial. However, partners are personally liable for business debts, and each partner is accountable for the actions of the others. This can lead to potential conflicts that might affect business operations. The partnership may also dissolve if a partner exits or passes away, unless there are agreements in place to handle such events.

A limited liability company (LLC) blends elements of both corporations and partnerships, offering a flexible and protective structure. Owners, known as members, are shielded from personal liability for business debts. LLCs have the flexibility to choose their tax classification, whether as a sole proprietorship, partnership, or corporation. This structure also demands fewer formalities and administrative requirements than a corporation. However, setting up an LLC is more costly than a sole proprietorship or partnership due to filing fees and ongoing compliance costs. There is also more paperwork and state-specific regulations to navigate, which can vary significantly and create complexities.

A corporation is a separate legal entity from its owners, providing the highest level of liability protection. Shareholders are not personally liable for corporate debts, and it is easier to raise capital through the sale of stock. Corporations enjoy perpetual existence, continuing even if ownership changes. On the downside, corporations are more complex and expensive to establish and maintain. They require extensive record-keeping, reporting, and compliance with regulatory requirements. Profits may be taxed twice—first at the corporate level and again as shareholder dividends, a scenario known as double taxation. Moreover, corporations must adhere to strict formalities and governance structures, including having a board of directors.

Selecting the appropriate business model is crucial for the success of your venture. Each structure has its unique advantages and disadvantages, impacting everything from your tax responsibilities to personal liability. By carefully considering these factors and seeking professional legal and financial advice, you can choose the business structure that best fits your goals and circumstances.

2 FINDING YOUR BUSINESS IDEA

Finding the right business idea is a crucial step in your entrepreneurial journey. It sets the foundation for everything that follows, from planning and funding to launching and growing your business. This chapter will guide you through identifying opportunities, spotting potential business ideas, and analyzing market needs and gaps.

Identifying Opportunities

Recognizing business opportunities involves a blend of creativity, market awareness, and strategic thinking. Here are some ways to spot promising opportunities:

How to Spot Business Opportunities

Stay curious and observant. Pay attention to everyday problems, inconveniences, and inefficiencies. Often, great business ideas stem from solutions to common issues. Talk to people, ask questions, and listen to their frustrations and suggestions.

Keep up with industry trends and emerging markets. Read industry publications, follow relevant blogs and news sources, and participate in industry events and conferences. Trends can highlight shifts in consumer behavior, technological advancements, and regulatory changes that might create new opportunities.

Leverage your skills and passions. Consider your own expertise, hobbies, and interests. A business idea rooted in something you are passionate about and skilled at is more likely to succeed and be fulfilling.

Network with other entrepreneurs and professionals. Join local business groups, attend networking events, and engage with online communities. Conversations with like-minded individuals can spark ideas and provide valuable insights.

Analyzing Market Needs and Gaps

Once you have a few potential ideas, the next step is to analyze the market to ensure there is a genuine need and a viable opportunity. Here's how you can do that:

Conduct market research. Gather data on your potential market, including size, demographics, and purchasing behavior. Use surveys, interviews, focus groups, and online research tools to gain insights into your target audience.

Identify gaps in the market. Look for areas where customer needs are not being fully met by existing products or services. This could be an underserved demographic, a missing feature, or an entirely new approach to solving a problem.

Evaluate the competition. Analyze existing businesses in your chosen market. Identify their strengths and weaknesses, and look for opportunities to differentiate your offering. Understanding your competition helps you refine your unique value proposition.

Test your idea. Before fully committing, test your concept with a small group of potential customers. Gather feedback, refine your idea, and assess whether there is a strong interest and willingness to pay for your product or service.

Consider scalability and sustainability. Ensure your business idea has the potential for growth and long-term viability. Assess the resources required, potential barriers to entry, and any legal or regulatory considerations.

Finding a business idea involves a mix of observation, research, and validation. By spotting opportunities and analyzing market needs and gaps, you can identify a viable and promising business concept. This foundation will prepare you for the next steps in your entrepreneurial journey, from developing a business plan to launching your venture.

Assessing Your Strengths and Interests

The next critical step in finding your business idea is to assess your strengths and interests. This self-assessment ensures that you choose a business that aligns with your skills and passions, increasing the likelihood of success and personal satisfaction.

Matching Your Skills and Passions with Business Ideas

Start by listing your skills, experiences, and areas of expertise. Reflect on your professional background, educational achievements, and personal hobbies. Consider what you enjoy doing and what you excel at. The intersection of your skills and passions is often the sweet spot for a successful business idea.

Think about how your skills can be applied to solve problems or meet needs in the market. For example, if you have a background in graphic design and a passion for sustainability, you might consider starting a business that offers eco-friendly packaging design services. The key is to find a business idea that leverages your strengths and aligns with what you love to do.

Evaluating Feasibility and Market Demand

After identifying a few potential business ideas that match your skills and passions, it's essential to evaluate their feasibility and market demand. This involves a deeper analysis to ensure that your idea is not only personally fulfilling but also commercially viable.

Begin by researching the market demand for your idea. Look for data on industry trends, customer needs, and potential competitors. Use tools like Google Trends, market reports, and social media insights to gauge interest and identify target demographics.

Assess the feasibility of your idea by considering factors such as startup costs, resource requirements, and potential challenges. Create a rough financial plan to estimate the initial investment needed and the expected revenue streams. Consider whether you have the necessary resources or if you will need to seek additional funding or partnerships.

Evaluate your idea's scalability and sustainability. Determine if the business can grow over time and adapt to changing market conditions. Consider the long-term potential and whether the market demand will remain stable or increase.

Gather feedback from potential customers or industry experts. Share your idea with a trusted network and seek constructive criticism. Use this feedback to refine your concept and address any potential issues.

By thoroughly assessing your strengths and interests and evaluating the feasibility and market demand, you can narrow down your options and choose a business idea that is both personally fulfilling and commercially viable. This careful consideration will set you up for success as you move forward in your entrepreneurial journey.

Validating Your Idea

Once you have a promising business idea that aligns with your strengths and interests, the next step is to validate it. Validation involves confirming that there is a real demand for your product or service and that your idea has the potential to succeed in the market. This process can save you time, money, and effort by ensuring that you pursue a viable opportunity.

Conducting Market Research

Start by conducting thorough market research to understand your target audience, industry trends, and competitive landscape. This research will help you gather crucial data to support your idea and refine your business strategy.

Begin with secondary research by reviewing existing market reports, industry publications, and online resources. Look for data on market size, growth projections, and key players in your industry. This information can provide valuable insights into the overall potential of your business idea.

Next, conduct primary research to gather firsthand information from your target audience. Use surveys, interviews, and focus groups to collect data on customer preferences, pain points, and buying behaviors. Ask specific questions related to your product or service to gauge interest and identify potential areas for improvement.

Analyze the data to identify patterns and trends. Look for indications that there is a substantial demand for your offering and that customers are willing to pay for it. This analysis will help you make informed decisions about how to position and market your business.

Gathering Feedback from Potential Customers

Gathering direct feedback from potential customers is a crucial step in validating your business idea. This feedback can provide valuable insights into how your target audience perceives your product or service and what improvements may be needed.

Start by creating a prototype or minimum viable product (MVP) that represents your idea. This doesn't have to be a fully developed product but should be enough to demonstrate its core features and value proposition. Share this prototype with a select group of potential customers and ask for their feedback.

Engage in conversations with your target audience through interviews, surveys, or informal discussions. Ask open-ended questions to understand their needs, preferences, and pain points. Pay attention to their reactions and suggestions, as this feedback can help you refine your idea and make necessary adjustments.

Consider using online platforms and social media to reach a broader audience. Create a landing page or social media campaign to showcase your idea and encourage feedback. Track engagement metrics such as likes, shares, comments, and sign-ups to gauge interest and collect valuable input.

Incorporate the feedback into your development process. Identify common themes and areas for improvement, and iterate on your idea to address these points. This iterative approach allows you to continually refine your product or service based on real-world feedback, increasing its chances of success.

By conducting thorough market research and gathering feedback from potential customers, you can validate your business idea and ensure it meets the needs of your target audience. This validation process provides a solid foundation for moving forward with confidence, knowing that your idea has the potential to succeed in the market.

3 DEVELOPING A BUSINESS PLAN

A well-crafted business plan is a crucial tool for any aspiring entrepreneur. It serves as a roadmap, guiding your journey from idea to reality and helping you stay focused and organized. This chapter explores the importance of a business plan and outlines its key components.

Importance of a Business Plan

Why You Need a Business Plan

A business plan is essential for several reasons. First and foremost, it provides clarity and direction. By outlining your goals, strategies, and actions, a business plan helps you stay on track and make informed decisions. It forces you to think critically about every aspect of your business, from market research and financial planning to marketing and operations.

A business plan is also a vital tool for securing funding. Investors and lenders want to see a clear, well-thought-out plan that demonstrates the viability and potential of your business. A comprehensive business plan shows that you have thoroughly researched your market, understand your competition, and have a solid strategy for success.

Additionally, a business plan helps you manage risk. By identifying potential challenges and outlining contingency plans, you can proactively address issues before they become critical. This preparation increases your chances of overcoming obstacles and achieving long-term success.

Key Components of a Business Plan

A robust business plan typically includes several key components, each serving a specific purpose. Here are the essential elements you should include:

Executive Summary

The executive summary is a brief overview of your business plan. It should highlight the main points, including your business concept, goals, target market, competitive advantage, and financial projections. Although it appears at the beginning of the plan, it's often written last, after you've detailed the other sections.

Company Description
This section provides a detailed description of your business. It includes your business name, structure (e.g., sole proprietorship, partnership, LLC), and location. You should also describe your mission statement, vision, and the products or services you offer. Explain what sets your business apart and why it will be successful.

Market Analysis
Conducting thorough market research is critical for understanding your industry, target market, and competition. In this section, present your findings, including market size, growth potential, and trends. Define your target audience and their needs, preferences, and behaviors. Analyze your competitors, highlighting their strengths and weaknesses, and explain how you plan to differentiate your business.

Organization and Management
Outline your business's organizational structure, including details about the ownership and management team. Provide information about the background and expertise of key team members, and describe their roles and responsibilities. This section should demonstrate that you have a capable and experienced team to execute your business plan.

Products or Services
Describe the products or services you will offer in detail. Explain the benefits and features, and how they meet the needs of your target market. Discuss your product lifecycle, including any plans for future development or innovation. Highlight any intellectual property, such as patents or trademarks, that provides a competitive edge.

Marketing and Sales Strategy
Your marketing and sales strategy outlines how you will attract and retain customers. Describe your pricing strategy, distribution channels, and promotional tactics. Explain how you will position your brand in the market and the key messages you will communicate. Include a sales strategy that details your sales process, techniques, and team structure.

Funding Request
If you are seeking funding, this section should clearly outline your requirements. Specify how much funding you need, the intended use of the funds, and any future financial needs. Provide details about your preferred funding type (e.g., equity, debt) and the terms you are seeking. This section

should be concise and persuasive, demonstrating the potential return on investment.

Financial Projections

Provide detailed financial forecasts, including income statements, cash flow statements, and balance sheets for the next three to five years. Include assumptions and explanations for your projections, and highlight any significant trends or factors influencing your financial outlook. This section should show that your business is financially viable and has growth potential.

Appendix

The appendix includes any additional information that supports your business plan, such as resumes of key team members, product images, legal documents, or detailed market research data. This section is optional but can provide valuable context and evidence to strengthen your plan.

A well-developed business plan is an invaluable tool that serves multiple purposes. It provides clarity and direction, helps secure funding, and prepares you to manage risks effectively. By including these key components, you can create a comprehensive and compelling business plan that sets the stage for your entrepreneurial success.

4 LEGAL STRUCTURE AND REQUIREMENTS

Selecting the appropriate legal structure is a fundamental decision for any new business. This choice affects your tax obligations, personal liability, and ability to raise capital, among other things. This chapter provides a detailed explanation of the different business structures and offers guidance on how to choose the right one for your business.

Choosing a Legal Structure
Detailed Explanation of Different Business Structures

Sole Proprietorship

A sole proprietorship is the simplest form of business structure. It is an unincorporated business owned and run by one individual, with no distinction between the owner and the business. This structure is easy to set up and offers complete control to the owner. However, the owner is personally liable for all business debts and obligations, which means personal assets are at risk if the business encounters financial trouble.

Partnership

A partnership involves two or more individuals who agree to share the profits and losses of a business. There are two main types of partnerships: general partnerships, where all partners are equally liable for the business's debts, and limited partnerships, where some partners have limited liability based on their investment in the business. Partnerships benefit from combined resources and skills, but like sole proprietorships, they come with personal liability for the owners.

Limited Liability Company (LLC)

An LLC is a hybrid structure that combines the liability protection of a corporation with the tax benefits and operational flexibility of a partnership. Owners of an LLC, known as members, are not personally liable for the business's debts and obligations. LLCs can choose to be taxed as a sole proprietorship, partnership, or corporation, which provides flexibility in how profits are distributed and taxed. However, LLCs can be more complex and expensive to establish than sole proprietorships or partnerships.

Corporation

A corporation is a legal entity separate from its owners, providing the highest level of liability protection. Shareholders are not personally liable for corporate debts, and the corporation can raise capital by issuing stock. There are different types of corporations, including C corporations and S corporations. C corporations face double taxation, where profits are taxed at the corporate level and again as shareholder dividends. S corporations avoid double taxation by passing income directly to shareholders, who report it on their personal tax returns. Corporations require more extensive record-keeping, reporting, and compliance with regulatory requirements.

How to Choose the Right Structure for Your Business

Choosing the right legal structure depends on various factors, including the nature of your business, your financial situation, and your long-term goals. Here are some key considerations to help you decide:

Liability Protection

Consider how much personal liability you are willing to assume. Sole proprietorships and general partnerships offer no personal liability protection, which means your personal assets could be at risk if your business incurs debt or is sued. LLCs and corporations provide liability protection, shielding your personal assets from business-related liabilities.

Tax Implications

Different structures have different tax implications. Sole proprietorships and partnerships pass profits directly to the owners, who report them on their personal tax returns. LLCs offer flexibility in taxation, allowing you to choose how you want to be taxed. Corporations, particularly C corporations, face double taxation, which might be a disadvantage for some businesses. Understanding these implications can help you choose a structure that aligns with your financial goals.

Cost and Complexity

Consider the cost and complexity of setting up and maintaining each structure. Sole proprietorships and partnerships are relatively easy and inexpensive to establish. LLCs and corporations involve more paperwork, regulatory requirements, and higher costs. Weigh these factors against the benefits each structure offers.

Control and Management

Think about how much control you want to retain over your business. Sole proprietorships and single-member LLCs allow for complete control by the owner. Partnerships and multi-member LLCs involve shared control, which requires clear agreements to manage decision-making. Corporations have a formal management structure with a board of directors, which can dilute your control.

Future Needs

Consider your long-term business goals. If you plan to scale your business, raise significant capital, or go public, a corporation might be the best choice. If you value flexibility and simplicity, an LLC could be more suitable. Your choice of structure should support your growth plans and business strategy.

Professional Advice

Consulting with legal and financial professionals can provide valuable insights tailored to your specific situation. They can help you understand the implications of each structure and guide you in making an informed decision.

Selecting the right legal structure is a crucial step in establishing a strong foundation for your business. By carefully considering liability protection, tax implications, cost, control, and future needs, you can choose the structure that best aligns with your goals and sets your business up for success.

Registering Your Business

Once you've chosen the appropriate legal structure for your business, the next step is to officially register your business. This process varies depending on your location and the type of business you're starting, but the following steps provide a general overview.

Steps to Register Your Business

Start by choosing a business name that is unique and not already in use by another business. Conduct a search in your state's business registry, as well as a trademark search to ensure your name is available and not trademarked by someone else.

Register your business name with the state or local government if required. Sole proprietorships and partnerships may need to file a "Doing Business As" (DBA) name, also known as a trade name or fictitious name, if the business name differs from the owner's legal name. LLCs and corporations will typically register their business name when they file their formation documents with the state.

Next, file the necessary formation documents for your business structure. For sole proprietorships, this step is often minimal, while partnerships may need a partnership agreement. LLCs must file Articles of Organization, and corporations need to file Articles of Incorporation with the appropriate state agency, usually the Secretary of State's office.

Obtain an Employer Identification Number (EIN) from the Internal Revenue Service (IRS). This unique number is used for tax purposes and is required for most businesses, especially those with employees or those that operate as a corporation or partnership. You can apply for an EIN online through the IRS website.

Register with state and local tax authorities. Depending on your location, you may need to register for state taxes, such as sales tax, payroll tax, or other specific business taxes. Contact your state's Department of Revenue or similar agency for detailed requirements.

Obtaining Necessary Licenses and Permits

After registering your business, you need to obtain the necessary licenses and permits to operate legally. The requirements vary depending on your industry, location, and business activities.

Research the specific licenses and permits required for your business type. Common examples include general business licenses, professional licenses, health permits, and zoning permits. Contact your local city or county government offices to determine what is needed.

Apply for the required licenses and permits through the appropriate local, state, or federal agencies. This process may involve submitting applications, paying fees, and meeting specific regulatory requirements. Ensure that you provide all the necessary documentation and information to avoid delays.

Stay compliant by renewing your licenses and permits as required. Many licenses and permits have expiration dates and must be renewed periodically. Keep track of renewal deadlines and maintain good standing with regulatory authorities to avoid fines or business interruptions.

Registering your business and obtaining the necessary licenses and permits are crucial steps in establishing a legal and compliant operation. By following these steps, you can ensure that your business is properly registered and authorized to operate, providing a solid foundation for growth and success.

Understanding Legal Obligations

Successfully running a business requires a thorough understanding of your legal obligations. These responsibilities encompass taxes, insurance, and various regulatory requirements. Ensuring compliance with these obligations is essential for maintaining good standing with authorities and protecting your business.

Taxes, Insurance, and Other Legal Requirements

Understanding your tax obligations is crucial. Your business structure will determine the types of taxes you need to pay. Sole proprietorships and partnerships report business income on personal tax returns, while corporations are taxed separately. LLCs can choose how they want to be taxed, either as a sole proprietorship, partnership, or corporation. In addition to federal taxes, you may also be responsible for state and local taxes, including income tax, sales tax, and employment taxes. It is important to register with the appropriate tax authorities and file returns on time to avoid penalties.

Insurance is another critical aspect of protecting your business. Depending on your industry and location, you may need several types of insurance. General liability insurance covers accidents and injuries on your business premises, while professional liability insurance protects against claims of negligence or malpractice. If you have employees, workers' compensation insurance is usually required by law. Additionally, property insurance covers damage to your business assets, and product liability insurance protects against claims related to your products.

Other legal requirements may include zoning regulations, health and safety standards, environmental regulations, and industry-specific laws. For example, restaurants must comply with health department regulations, while manufacturers may need to meet environmental protection standards. Familiarize yourself with the regulations that apply to your business and ensure you meet all necessary requirements.

Importance of Compliance and Record-Keeping

Maintaining compliance with legal obligations is not only a legal necessity but also a good business practice. Compliance helps you avoid fines, legal disputes, and potential shutdowns. It also enhances your business's reputation, building trust with customers, investors, and partners.

Record-keeping is a fundamental part of compliance. Accurate and organized records provide a clear picture of your business activities and financial health. Keep detailed records of income, expenses, payroll, and tax filings. This documentation is essential for preparing financial statements, filing taxes, and supporting claims during audits.

Implement a system for regular record-keeping. Use accounting software to track financial transactions and generate reports. Ensure that all receipts, invoices, contracts, and other important documents are stored securely and are easily accessible. Regularly back up digital records to prevent data loss.

Stay informed about changes in laws and regulations that may affect your business. Subscribe to industry newsletters, attend workshops, and consult with legal and financial advisors to keep up-to-date with new requirements. Periodically review your compliance practices and make adjustments as necessary.

By understanding your legal obligations and the importance of compliance and record-keeping, you can protect your business from legal issues and establish a strong foundation for growth. Ensuring that your business meets all legal requirements will enable you to focus on achieving your entrepreneurial goals with confidence and peace of mind.

5 FINANCING YOUR BUSINESS

Securing the necessary funds to start and grow your business is one of the most critical steps in the entrepreneurial journey. Proper financial planning ensures that you have the resources needed to turn your vision into reality. This chapter will guide you through estimating startup costs and creating a budget to manage your finances effectively.

Estimating Startup Costs

Identifying and Calculating Initial Expenses

Before you can secure financing, you need a clear understanding of the costs involved in launching your business. Start by identifying all potential expenses associated with your business. These can be categorized into several key areas:

Business Registration and Licenses: These include fees for registering your business name, obtaining necessary permits, and any legal costs associated with setting up your business structure.

Equipment and Supplies: Consider the costs of purchasing or leasing equipment, furniture, office supplies, and technology. This might include computers, software, machinery, or any specialized tools required for your operations.

Location and Utilities: If you need a physical location, factor in the costs of leasing or purchasing property, as well as utility expenses such as electricity, water, and internet services.

Marketing and Advertising: Initial marketing expenses can include website development, branding materials, social media campaigns, and other promotional activities to attract your first customers.

Inventory: For product-based businesses, calculate the cost of initial inventory, including raw materials, finished goods, and any storage costs.

Employee Salaries and Benefits: If you plan to hire staff, estimate the costs of salaries, benefits, and any other employee-related expenses such as recruitment and training.

Professional Services: This includes fees for accountants, lawyers, consultants, and any other professional services you may require during the startup phase.

Operational Costs: Consider day-to-day operational expenses such as insurance, maintenance, and office supplies. Also, include any costs related to setting up your business processes and systems.

To calculate these expenses, research and gather quotes from suppliers, service providers, and landlords. Be thorough and realistic in your estimations, and consider adding a buffer for unexpected costs. Creating a detailed list of all potential expenses will provide a clear picture of the funds needed to start your business.

Creating a Budget

Once you have identified and calculated your initial expenses, the next step is to create a budget. A budget is a financial plan that outlines your expected income and expenses, helping you manage your cash flow and ensure you have enough funds to cover your costs.

Start by categorizing your expenses into fixed and variable costs. Fixed costs are those that remain constant regardless of your business activity, such as rent, salaries, and insurance. Variable costs fluctuate with your level of production or sales, such as inventory purchases, shipping costs, and marketing expenses.

Estimate your projected revenue based on market research and sales forecasts. This will help you determine how much capital you need to break even and become profitable. Be conservative in your revenue estimates to account for uncertainties and potential delays in reaching your sales targets.

Create a monthly budget for the first year of operations, detailing your expected income and expenses for each month. This will help you track your financial performance and make adjustments as needed. Include a cash flow statement to monitor the inflow and outflow of cash, ensuring you have enough liquidity to cover your expenses.

Review and adjust your budget regularly. As you gain more experience and gather actual financial data, update your budget to reflect changes in your business environment and operations. This will help you stay on top of your finances and make informed decisions.

Properly estimating startup costs and creating a detailed budget are essential steps in securing financing and managing your business's financial health. By understanding your financial needs and planning accordingly, you can ensure that you have the resources to launch and sustain your business, paving the way for long-term success.

Funding Options

Securing adequate funding is crucial for turning your business idea into a reality. There are several ways to finance your startup, each with its own advantages and considerations. Understanding these options can help you choose the best approach for your business needs.

Self-Funding

Self-funding, also known as bootstrapping, involves using your personal savings or assets to finance your business. This method allows you to maintain full control and ownership of your business without incurring debt or giving away equity.

One of the main advantages of self-funding is that it demonstrates your commitment to your business, which can be appealing to potential investors or lenders down the line. However, using personal funds can be risky, as it involves putting your personal financial security on the line. It's essential to carefully assess your financial situation and ensure you have enough savings to cover both your business and personal expenses.

Loans and Credit

Business loans and lines of credit are common ways to finance a startup. These options allow you to borrow money that must be repaid over time with interest.

Banks and credit unions offer various loan products tailored to small businesses, including term loans, which provide a lump sum that is repaid over a set period, and lines of credit, which offer flexible access to funds as needed. To qualify for a loan, you typically need a solid business plan, good credit history, and collateral to secure the loan.

While loans provide the capital needed to start and grow your business, they come with the obligation of repayment and interest, which can strain your cash flow. It's important to carefully evaluate the terms and ensure you can meet the repayment requirements.

Investors and Venture Capital

For businesses with high growth potential, seeking investment from angel investors or venture capitalists (VCs) can be a viable option. Investors provide capital in exchange for equity in your business, meaning they will own a share of your company.

Angel investors are typically individuals who invest their own money in early-stage startups, often in exchange for convertible debt or ownership equity. They may also provide mentorship and valuable industry connections.

Venture capitalists are professional groups that manage pooled funds from many investors to invest in high-potential startups. VC funding often comes in larger amounts than angel investment and may be provided in multiple rounds as your business grows.

The primary advantage of securing investment is that you gain substantial funding without the need for immediate repayment. However, giving up equity means sharing ownership and control of your business. Investors may also expect significant returns on their investment, which can add pressure to achieve rapid growth.

Crowdfunding and Grants

Crowdfunding is a method of raising small amounts of money from a large number of people, typically through online platforms such as Kickstarter, Indiegogo, or GoFundMe. This approach allows you to present your business idea to the public and attract funds from supporters who believe in your vision.

Crowdfunding can be a powerful way to validate your business idea and build a community of early adopters. However, successful crowdfunding campaigns require significant effort in marketing and communication to reach and engage potential backers.

Grants are non-repayable funds provided by governments, non-profits, and private organizations to support businesses, particularly those that align with specific social, economic, or technological goals. Grants can be an excellent source of funding as they do not require repayment or equity.

To secure a grant, you must meet the eligibility criteria and often undergo a competitive application process. The requirements and availability of grants vary widely, so it's important to research and apply for grants that fit your business model and objectives.

Each funding option has its own set of advantages and challenges. By carefully considering your business needs, growth potential, and risk tolerance, you can select the best funding strategy to support your entrepreneurial journey. Understanding these options will equip you with the knowledge to make informed financial decisions and secure the resources necessary for your business's success.

Managing Finances

Proper financial management is critical for the success and sustainability of your business. This involves setting up appropriate financial systems, keeping accurate records, and regularly reviewing your financial performance. Here are the essential steps to effectively manage your business finances.

Setting Up a Business Bank Account

The first step in managing your finances is to separate your personal and business finances by setting up a dedicated business bank account. This separation is crucial for accurate record-keeping, legal protection, and simplifying tax preparation.

Choose a bank that offers favorable terms and services tailored to small businesses. When opening an account, you may need to provide documentation such as your business registration, employer identification number (EIN), and personal identification. A business bank account allows you to manage your income and expenses more efficiently and provides a clear financial trail, which is essential for auditing and legal purposes.

Basics of Bookkeeping and Accounting

Effective bookkeeping and accounting practices are the backbone of your financial management system. Bookkeeping involves recording daily financial transactions, while accounting involves summarizing, analyzing, and reporting these transactions.

Start by choosing the right accounting method for your business. The two main methods are cash accounting, where transactions are recorded when cash is received or paid, and accrual accounting, where transactions are recorded when they are earned or incurred, regardless of cash flow. Most small businesses use cash accounting for its simplicity, but accrual accounting provides a more accurate financial picture.

Invest in accounting software to streamline your bookkeeping process. These tools can help you track income and expenses, generate invoices, and manage payroll. Popular options include QuickBooks, Xero, and FreshBooks. Alternatively, you can hire a professional bookkeeper or accountant to handle these tasks, ensuring accuracy and compliance with tax regulations.

Maintain detailed records of all financial transactions, including sales, purchases, payments, and receipts. Organize documents systematically, either digitally or physically, to ensure they are easily accessible when needed. Regularly reconcile your accounts to verify that your records match your bank statements, identifying and resolving discrepancies promptly.

Financial Statements and Cash Flow Management

Regularly reviewing financial statements is essential for understanding your business's financial health and making informed decisions. The three primary financial statements you need to monitor are the income statement, balance sheet, and cash flow statement.

The income statement, also known as the profit and loss statement, shows your revenue, expenses, and profits over a specific period. This statement helps you assess your business's profitability and identify trends in your income and expenses.

The balance sheet provides a snapshot of your business's financial position at a given point in time. It lists your assets, liabilities, and equity, showing what your business owns and owes. The balance sheet helps you evaluate your business's net worth and financial stability.

The cash flow statement tracks the movement of cash in and out of your business. It highlights your operational, investing, and financing activities, helping you manage liquidity and ensure you have enough cash to cover your obligations.

Effective cash flow management is crucial for maintaining your business's solvency. Monitor your cash flow regularly to identify patterns and anticipate shortages. Implement strategies to improve cash flow, such as speeding up receivables, managing inventory efficiently, and negotiating favorable payment terms with suppliers.

Create a cash flow forecast to project your future cash inflows and outflows. This forecast helps you plan for periods of surplus or deficit, allowing you to take proactive measures such as securing a line of credit or adjusting your expenses.

By setting up a business bank account, maintaining accurate bookkeeping and accounting practices, and regularly reviewing your financial statements and cash flow, you can effectively manage your business finances. These steps will help you stay financially healthy, make informed decisions, and achieve long-term success.

6 BUILDING YOUR BRAND

Building a strong brand is essential for distinguishing your business in the marketplace and creating a lasting impression on your customers. A well-defined brand identity communicates who you are, what you stand for, and why customers should choose you over competitors. This chapter will guide you through the process of creating a brand identity, emphasizing the importance of branding and the steps to develop a compelling brand name, logo, and tagline.

Creating a Brand Identity

Importance of Branding
Branding is more than just a logo or a catchy tagline; it encompasses the entire experience your customers have with your business. A strong brand creates a sense of trust, loyalty, and emotional connection with your audience. Here are a few reasons why branding is crucial for your business:

First, branding helps differentiate your business in a crowded marketplace. With so many products and services competing for attention, a unique brand identity makes your business stand out and attracts your target audience.

Second, branding builds recognition and trust. Consistent branding across all touchpoints, from your website to social media profiles, helps customers easily recognize and remember your business. Trust is established when customers know what to expect from your brand, leading to increased loyalty and repeat business.

Third, a strong brand can justify premium pricing. When customers perceive your brand as high-quality or exclusive, they are often willing to pay more for your products or services. This can significantly enhance your profitability.

Lastly, branding supports your marketing efforts. A clear and compelling brand identity provides a solid foundation for all your marketing activities, ensuring consistency and effectiveness in your messaging.

Developing a Brand Name, Logo, and Tagline

The first step in creating a brand identity is developing a memorable brand name. Your brand name should reflect your business's values, personality, and the products or services you offer. It should be easy to pronounce, spell, and remember. Conduct thorough research to ensure your chosen name is unique and not already in use by another business. Consider testing your name with potential customers to gather feedback and ensure it resonates with your target audience.

Once you have a brand name, the next step is to create a logo. A logo is a visual representation of your brand and plays a critical role in establishing your identity. Work with a professional designer to create a logo that is simple, versatile, and reflective of your brand's essence. Your logo should be scalable, working well in different sizes and across various media, from business cards to billboards. Choose colors, fonts, and shapes that convey the right message and evoke the desired emotions in your audience.

In addition to a brand name and logo, develop a compelling tagline. A tagline is a short, memorable phrase that captures the essence of your brand and communicates your unique value proposition. It should be concise, clear, and impactful, leaving a lasting impression on your audience. A well-crafted tagline reinforces your brand message and enhances brand recall.

Building a cohesive brand identity involves more than just creating a name, logo, and tagline. It requires a consistent visual and verbal style across all your marketing materials. Develop brand guidelines that outline your brand's color palette, typography, imagery, and tone of voice. These guidelines ensure that everyone in your organization communicates your brand consistently, whether through social media posts, advertising campaigns, or customer service interactions.

Creating a strong brand identity is an ongoing process that evolves with your business. Regularly review and refine your branding to ensure it stays relevant and resonates with your audience. Engage with your customers to gather feedback and understand their perceptions of your brand. This continuous improvement will help you maintain a strong brand presence and foster long-term relationships with your customers.

By understanding the importance of branding and following the steps to develop a brand name, logo, and tagline, you can create a powerful brand identity that differentiates your business, builds trust, and drives customer loyalty. A well-crafted brand identity sets the foundation for all your marketing efforts and contributes significantly to your business's success.

Establishing an Online Presence

In today's digital age, establishing an online presence is crucial for any business. Your online presence not only helps you reach a broader audience but also enhances your brand's credibility and accessibility. Here are key steps to building a robust online presence through a website and social media.

Building a Website

Your website is often the first point of contact between your business and potential customers. It serves as your digital storefront, providing information about your products or services, and reflecting your brand's identity. Here's how to build an effective website:

First, choose a domain name that is easy to remember and closely related to your brand name. Ensure the domain is available and consider registering variations to protect your brand.

Select a reliable web hosting service to ensure your website is always accessible. There are various hosting options available, from shared hosting to dedicated servers, depending on your needs and budget.

Design your website with your target audience in mind. A professional, user-friendly design enhances the user experience and encourages visitors to stay longer. Focus on intuitive navigation, clear calls to action, and a responsive design that works well on all devices.

Your website should effectively communicate your brand's value proposition. Include essential pages such as Home, About Us, Products/Services, Contact, and Blog. Each page should have compelling content that aligns with your brand voice and provides value to your visitors.

Optimize your website for search engines (SEO) to improve its visibility. Use relevant keywords, meta tags, and high-quality content to attract organic traffic. Regularly update your website with fresh content to keep it engaging and improve search rankings.

Incorporate analytics tools to track visitor behavior and gather insights. Tools like Google Analytics help you understand your audience's preferences and improve your website's performance.

Utilizing Social Media

Social media platforms are powerful tools for building your brand and engaging with your audience. Here's how to effectively utilize social media for your business:

Identify the social media platforms that are most popular with your target audience. Common platforms include Facebook, Instagram, Twitter, LinkedIn, and Pinterest. Focus your efforts on a few key platforms to maximize impact.

Create consistent, high-quality content that reflects your brand's identity and values. This content can include blog posts, images, videos, infographics, and user-generated content. Ensure that your posts are visually appealing and shareable.

Engage with your audience regularly. Respond to comments, messages, and reviews promptly and professionally. Building a community around your brand involves active participation and genuine interaction with your followers.

Use social media to share updates, promotions, and news about your business. Highlight new products, special offers, and events to keep your audience informed and engaged.

Leverage social media advertising to reach a broader audience. Platforms like Facebook and Instagram offer targeted advertising options that allow you to reach specific demographics based on interests, location, and behavior. Invest in ads to increase your brand's visibility and drive traffic to your website.

Monitor your social media performance using analytics tools provided by each platform. Track metrics such as engagement rates, follower growth, and website traffic to understand what's working and adjust your strategy accordingly.

Collaborate with influencers and industry leaders to expand your reach. Influencers can help you tap into new audiences and build credibility. Choose influencers whose values align with your brand and who have a genuine connection with their followers.

Maintaining a strong online presence through a well-designed website and active social media engagement is vital for modern businesses. By creating a user-friendly website and leveraging social media platforms, you can effectively communicate your brand's value, engage with your audience, and drive business growth. A robust online presence not only enhances your brand's visibility but also builds trust and fosters long-term relationships with your customers.

Marketing and Advertising

Effectively marketing and advertising your business is crucial for attracting customers and driving sales. As a beginner, understanding the differences between traditional and digital marketing, and implementing effective strategies, will help you maximize your reach and impact.

Traditional vs. Digital Marketing

Traditional marketing encompasses methods that have been used for decades to reach a broad audience. This includes print media (newspapers, magazines, brochures), broadcast media (television, radio), direct mail, and outdoor advertising (billboards, posters). Traditional marketing can be very effective for local businesses or those targeting a broad demographic. It often involves higher costs and requires more time to measure its impact compared to digital marketing.

Digital marketing leverages online platforms and technologies to promote products and services. This includes search engine marketing (SEM), social media marketing, email marketing, content marketing, and pay-per-click (PPC) advertising. Digital marketing offers several advantages, such as lower costs, precise targeting, real-time analytics, and the ability to engage directly with customers. It's particularly effective for reaching specific audiences and can be adjusted quickly based on performance data.

Effective Marketing Strategies for Beginners

As a beginner, starting with a clear marketing strategy will help you use your resources efficiently and achieve your business goals. Here are some effective strategies to consider:

Define Your Target Audience

Understanding your target audience is the foundation of any marketing strategy. Conduct market research to identify the demographics, interests, and behaviors of your ideal customers. Knowing who you are targeting allows you to tailor your marketing messages and choose the right channels to reach them.

Create a Strong Brand Message

Develop a compelling brand message that clearly communicates your unique value proposition. This message should highlight what sets your business apart from competitors and why customers should choose you. Consistency in your brand message across all marketing channels builds recognition and trust.

Utilize Social Media

Leverage social media platforms to connect with your audience and promote your business. Choose the platforms that your target audience uses the most and create engaging content that resonates with them. Use a mix of posts, stories, and live videos to keep your audience interested. Engage with your followers by responding to comments and messages, and encourage user-generated content to increase authenticity and trust.

Content Marketing

Create valuable content that addresses the needs and interests of your target audience. This can include blog posts, videos, infographics, and podcasts. Content marketing not only helps attract and engage potential customers but also improves your search engine rankings. Regularly update your content to keep it fresh and relevant.

Email Marketing

Build an email list and use email marketing to nurture relationships with your customers. Send regular newsletters with updates, promotions, and valuable content. Personalize your emails to make them more relevant to the recipients. Email marketing is an effective way to keep your audience informed and encourage repeat business.

Search Engine Optimization (SEO)

Optimize your website for search engines to increase organic traffic. Use relevant keywords, meta tags, and high-quality content to improve your search engine rankings. SEO is a long-term strategy that helps your business become more visible to potential customers who are searching for products or services like yours.

Pay-Per-Click (PPC) Advertising

Invest in PPC advertising to drive immediate traffic to your website. Platforms like Google Ads and social media sites offer PPC options that allow you to target specific audiences with precision. Set a budget and monitor your campaigns to ensure you get a good return on investment.

Local Marketing

If you have a local business, focus on local marketing strategies. This includes optimizing your Google My Business profile, getting listed in local directories, and participating in community events. Local marketing helps you attract customers in your immediate area and build a loyal customer base.

Measure and Adjust

Track the performance of your marketing efforts using analytics tools. Monitor key metrics such as website traffic, conversion rates, social media engagement, and email open rates. Use this data to evaluate the effectiveness of your strategies and make necessary adjustments. Continuous monitoring and optimization help you improve your marketing results over time.

By understanding the differences between traditional and digital marketing and implementing effective strategies, you can build a strong marketing foundation for your business. Tailoring your approach to your target audience and continuously refining your efforts will help you attract and retain customers, ultimately driving your business's growth and success.

7 SETTING UP YOUR BUSINESS OPERATIONS

Setting up your business operations is a critical step in ensuring your business runs smoothly and efficiently. This chapter focuses on establishing a solid foundation through careful selection of your business location and setting up an effective workspace.

Location and Infrastructure

Choosing a Business Location

The location of your business can significantly impact its success. Whether you're opening a retail store, a restaurant, or an office, choosing the right location is crucial. Here are some factors to consider:

First, understand your target market and choose a location that is convenient for them. Analyze the demographics of the area to ensure it aligns with your target audience. For example, a boutique targeting young professionals might thrive in a trendy urban area, while a family restaurant might do better in a suburban neighborhood.

Accessibility is another critical factor. Ensure your location is easily accessible by public transportation and has ample parking if necessary. High foot traffic areas can be beneficial for retail businesses, as they attract more customers.

Consider the competition in the area. Being close to competitors can be advantageous if it draws more customers to the area, but it can also be challenging if the market is saturated. Analyze the strengths and weaknesses of nearby businesses to determine if your business can compete effectively.

Evaluate the cost of the location, including rent, utilities, and any additional expenses such as property taxes and maintenance. Ensure that these costs fit within your budget without compromising other critical areas of your business.

Check local zoning laws and regulations to ensure your business type is permitted in the area. Obtain any necessary permits and licenses before committing to a location.

Setting Up Your Workspace

Creating a productive and efficient workspace is essential for the smooth operation of your business. Whether you're setting up a home office, a retail store, or a large corporate office, here are key considerations:

Design your workspace layout to enhance productivity and workflow. Arrange workstations, equipment, and storage areas in a way that minimizes movement and maximizes efficiency. For a retail store, ensure that the layout is customer-friendly and encourages browsing and purchases.

Invest in quality furniture and equipment that meets the needs of your business and employees. Ergonomic chairs, desks, and workstations can improve comfort and productivity. Ensure you have all necessary technology, such as computers, printers, and communication tools, to support your operations.

Consider the aesthetics of your workspace. A well-designed and visually appealing workspace can boost employee morale and create a positive impression on customers and clients. Choose a color scheme and décor that reflect your brand identity and create a welcoming atmosphere.

Ensure your workspace meets health and safety standards. This includes proper ventilation, adequate lighting, and adherence to fire and building codes. Regularly inspect and maintain your equipment and facilities to prevent accidents and ensure a safe working environment.

Set up efficient systems for organization and storage. Use filing cabinets, shelves, and digital storage solutions to keep documents and supplies organized and easily accessible. Implement a system for managing inventory if applicable to your business.

Incorporate areas for collaboration and relaxation. Designate spaces where employees can meet, brainstorm, and take breaks. This fosters a positive work environment and encourages teamwork and creativity.

Plan for future growth. Choose a location and design a workspace that can accommodate your business's growth. This might involve selecting a larger space than initially needed or choosing a location with expansion options.

By carefully choosing a business location and setting up an effective workspace, you lay the groundwork for efficient and successful operations. These steps are crucial for creating a productive environment that supports your business goals and provides a positive experience for both employees and customers. With a well-thought-out location and workspace, your business is better positioned for long-term success and growth.

Hiring and Managing Employees

Employees are the backbone of your business. Recruiting the right talent and effectively managing and training them are essential for building a strong, capable team that can drive your business toward success. This section will guide you through the process of hiring and managing employees to ensure your business operates smoothly and efficiently.

Recruiting the Right Talent

The first step in building a successful team is recruiting the right talent. Begin by clearly defining the roles you need to fill and the skills required for each position. Write detailed job descriptions that outline the responsibilities, qualifications, and expectations for each role.

Next, advertise the job openings through various channels. Utilize online job boards, social media, and your company website to reach a wide audience. Consider reaching out to professional networks and industry associations to find candidates with specialized skills.

Conduct a thorough screening process to identify the most qualified candidates. Review resumes and cover letters to assess their experience and skills. Conduct initial phone interviews to narrow down the pool of applicants and gain a better understanding of their qualifications and fit for your company.

Once you have a shortlist of candidates, conduct in-person or video interviews to delve deeper into their experience and capabilities. Use behavioral interview questions to assess how they have handled situations in the past and how they might perform in your company. Check references to verify their work history and gain insights into their work ethic and performance.

Evaluate candidates not only for their skills and experience but also for their cultural fit with your company. A candidate who aligns with your company's values and culture is more likely to thrive and contribute positively to your team.

Employee Management and Training

After hiring the right talent, effective management and training are crucial to ensure your employees perform at their best and contribute to your business's success.

Start with a comprehensive onboarding process to help new employees integrate into your company. Provide an orientation that covers your company's mission, values, policies, and procedures. Introduce them to their team members and provide the necessary tools and resources to start their job.

Create clear and achievable performance goals for each employee. Set expectations and provide regular feedback to help them understand how they are performing and where they can improve. Use performance reviews to formally assess their progress and identify opportunities for development.

Invest in employee training and development to enhance their skills and knowledge. Offer ongoing training programs, workshops, and access to industry conferences. Encourage employees to pursue certifications and further education related to their roles.

Foster a positive work environment by recognizing and rewarding employees for their contributions. Implement recognition programs, such as employee of the month awards, and offer incentives such as bonuses, promotions, and additional responsibilities for outstanding performance.

Promote open communication and create a culture of transparency. Encourage employees to share their ideas, concerns, and feedback. Regular team meetings and one-on-one check-ins can help maintain open lines of communication and address any issues promptly.

Support employee well-being by providing a healthy work-life balance. Offer flexible work schedules, remote work options, and employee wellness programs. Show empathy and understanding for personal issues and provide support when needed.

Implement effective conflict resolution strategies to address any disputes or issues that arise within the team. Address conflicts promptly and fairly, ensuring all parties are heard and a resolution is reached that aligns with your company's policies and values.

By focusing on recruiting the right talent and providing effective management and training, you can build a dedicated and high-performing team. A strong team not only enhances productivity and efficiency but also fosters a positive and collaborative work environment. Investing in your employees' growth and well-being will contribute to the long-term success and sustainability of your business.

Creating Efficient Processes

Efficiency is key to the smooth operation and growth of your business. Establishing streamlined workflows and leveraging technology can significantly enhance productivity, reduce costs, and improve overall performance. This section explores how to create efficient processes through effective workflow and operations management, as well as the utilization of technology and software.

Workflow and Operations Management

Creating efficient workflows begins with a clear understanding of your business operations. Start by mapping out all the processes involved in your business, from product development and procurement to sales and customer service. Identify each step in these processes and determine the best sequence to maximize efficiency.

Standardize your procedures by developing detailed process documentation. This includes creating step-by-step guides, checklists, and templates that employees can follow to ensure consistency and accuracy in their work. Standardization helps minimize errors, reduces training time, and ensures that all employees are working towards the same standards.

Implement project management techniques to keep track of tasks and deadlines. Use project management tools to assign responsibilities, monitor progress, and ensure that projects are completed on time and within budget.

Regularly review your processes to identify bottlenecks or inefficiencies and make adjustments as needed.

Encourage a culture of continuous improvement. Regularly solicit feedback from employees on the effectiveness of current processes and encourage them to suggest improvements. Hold regular process review meetings to discuss potential changes and implement the best ideas.

Optimize your supply chain management to ensure smooth and timely delivery of goods and services. Develop strong relationships with suppliers and negotiate favorable terms. Monitor inventory levels closely to avoid stockouts or excess inventory, and use demand forecasting to plan for future needs.

Utilizing Technology and Software

Technology plays a vital role in enhancing business efficiency. Utilize software and digital tools to automate routine tasks, streamline operations, and improve communication. Here are some key areas where technology can make a significant impact:

Implement enterprise resource planning (ERP) systems to integrate all aspects of your business operations, including inventory management, accounting, human resources, and customer relationship management (CRM). An ERP system provides a centralized platform to manage and analyze data, improving decision-making and operational efficiency.

Use accounting software to automate financial tasks such as invoicing, payroll, and expense tracking. This reduces the risk of errors, saves time, and ensures accurate financial records. Popular accounting software options include QuickBooks, Xero, and FreshBooks.

Leverage customer relationship management (CRM) software to manage interactions with customers and prospects. A CRM system helps you track customer inquiries, sales activities, and support requests, enabling you to provide personalized service and build stronger customer relationships. Examples of CRM software include Salesforce, HubSpot, and Zoho CRM.

Adopt project management and collaboration tools to enhance team productivity and coordination. Tools like Asana, Trello, and Slack allow teams to manage tasks, share files, and communicate in real-time, ensuring everyone is aligned and projects progress smoothly.

Utilize e-commerce platforms and digital payment systems to streamline online sales and transactions. Platforms like Shopify, WooCommerce, and Stripe make it easy to set up an online store, process payments securely, and manage orders efficiently.

Invest in marketing automation tools to streamline your marketing efforts. Tools like Mailchimp, Hootsuite, and Buffer allow you to schedule social media posts, send automated email campaigns, and analyze marketing performance. Automation frees up time and ensures consistent and timely communication with your audience.

Ensure data security and backup solutions are in place to protect your business information. Use cloud storage services like Google Drive, Dropbox, or Microsoft OneDrive to store and share files securely. Implement regular data backups and cybersecurity measures to safeguard against data loss and breaches.

By creating efficient workflows and utilizing technology, you can significantly enhance the operational efficiency of your business. These steps not only improve productivity and reduce costs but also enable you to scale your operations more effectively. Embracing a culture of continuous improvement and staying updated with the latest technological advancements will keep your business agile and competitive in an ever-evolving market.

8 LAUNCHING YOUR BUSINESS

Launching your business is an exciting milestone, marking the transition from planning to execution. A successful launch requires careful preparation and a well-thought-out plan to ensure everything goes smoothly. This chapter will guide you through the essential steps to prepare for your business launch and create a comprehensive launch plan.

Preparing for Launch

Final Checklist Before Launching
Before opening your doors to customers, it's crucial to ensure that all aspects of your business are ready. Here's a final checklist to help you prepare for launch day:
First, verify that all legal and regulatory requirements have been met. Ensure that your business is properly registered, licenses and permits are obtained, and any necessary inspections have been completed.
Ensure that your business location and workspace are fully set up. This includes having all necessary equipment, furniture, and supplies in place. Test all systems, such as POS systems, internet connections, and phone lines, to ensure they are functioning correctly.
Stock up on inventory and materials needed for your operations. Ensure that you have sufficient stock to meet initial demand and that your supply chain is prepared to handle ongoing needs.
Finalize your branding and marketing materials. Ensure that your website is live and fully functional, social media profiles are set up, and marketing collateral such as brochures, business cards, and signage are ready.
Train your employees thoroughly. Ensure that everyone understands their roles, responsibilities, and the procedures they need to follow. Conduct final training sessions on customer service, product knowledge, and any other relevant areas.
Test your processes and systems. Run through scenarios such as customer interactions, sales transactions, and order fulfillments to identify and address

any issues. This will help you ensure that everything operates smoothly on launch day.

Plan for contingencies. Prepare for potential issues that might arise, such as supply chain disruptions, technical problems, or unexpected high demand. Having a contingency plan in place will help you respond effectively to any challenges.

Creating a Launch Plan

A detailed launch plan is essential to coordinate all activities and ensure a successful launch. Here's how to create an effective launch plan:

Start by setting clear goals for your launch. Determine what you want to achieve, such as sales targets, customer acquisition goals, or brand awareness milestones. Having specific, measurable objectives will help you gauge the success of your launch.

Develop a timeline leading up to the launch date. Outline key activities and milestones, such as finalizing inventory, completing marketing campaigns, and conducting staff training. Assign responsibilities and deadlines to ensure that everyone knows what needs to be done and when.

Plan your marketing and promotional activities. Create a marketing campaign that generates excitement and anticipation for your launch. This can include social media teasers, email marketing, press releases, and special promotions. Consider hosting a launch event, such as a grand opening or an online live event, to attract attention and drive engagement.

Prepare your sales and customer service strategies. Train your team on how to handle inquiries, process transactions, and resolve issues. Ensure that your sales channels, both online and offline, are ready to handle orders and provide a seamless customer experience.

Coordinate with suppliers and partners. Ensure that your suppliers are aware of your launch timeline and can meet your inventory needs. Communicate with any partners or collaborators to align efforts and maximize the impact of your launch.

Set up tracking and analytics to monitor the success of your launch. Use tools to track website traffic, social media engagement, sales figures, and customer feedback. This data will help you evaluate the effectiveness of your launch activities and make necessary adjustments.

Prepare post-launch activities. Plan follow-up marketing campaigns to maintain momentum after the initial launch. Engage with your customers through email newsletters, social media updates, and special offers to keep them interested and encourage repeat business.

By thoroughly preparing for your business launch and creating a comprehensive launch plan, you can ensure a smooth and successful introduction to the market. A well-executed launch sets the stage for your business's growth and success, helping you build a strong foundation and make a positive first impression on your customers.

Executing the Launch

Once your preparations are complete and your launch plan is in place, it's time to execute the launch of your business. This involves carrying out your marketing and promotional activities and ensuring that launch day events run smoothly. A well-executed launch can generate significant buzz, attract customers, and set the tone for your business's future success.

Marketing and Promotional Activities

Effective marketing and promotional activities are crucial to generating excitement and driving traffic to your business on launch day. Here's how to execute these activities:

Begin by implementing your marketing campaign across all chosen channels. Utilize social media platforms to create a buzz around your launch. Share engaging content such as behind-the-scenes looks, product teasers, countdowns, and promotional offers. Use targeted ads to reach your specific audience and increase visibility.

Leverage email marketing to inform your existing contacts about the launch. Send out a series of emails leading up to the launch, providing details about your business, the launch event, and any special promotions. Offer exclusive discounts or early access to your email subscribers to create a sense of exclusivity and urgency.

Engage with local media and influencers to amplify your reach. Send press releases to local newspapers, magazines, and online publications to announce your launch. Invite influential bloggers, social media personalities, and industry experts to your launch event and encourage them to share their experiences with their followers.

Consider running limited-time promotions to attract customers. Offer special discounts, bundle deals, or freebies for the first few customers or during the launch period. These promotions can incentivize people to visit your business and make purchases.

Utilize content marketing to provide valuable information and attract potential customers. Publish blog posts, videos, and infographics that highlight the benefits of your products or services. Ensure that this content is optimized for search engines to increase organic traffic to your website.

Launch Day Activities and Events

The activities and events you plan for launch day can make a significant impact on your initial customer engagement and long-term success. Here's how to ensure a successful launch day:

Start by creating a welcoming and festive atmosphere at your business location. Decorate your space with banners, balloons, and signage that highlight the launch. Play upbeat music and create a lively environment that attracts passersby and invites them to come in.

Ensure that your staff is well-prepared and enthusiastic. Brief your team on their roles and responsibilities for the day, and encourage them to provide excellent customer service. Having a friendly, knowledgeable team can make a positive impression on your customers.

Host a launch event to draw attention and attract visitors. This could be a grand opening ceremony, a ribbon-cutting event, or a special in-store experience. Offer refreshments, conduct product demonstrations, and organize activities or entertainment to keep attendees engaged.

Capture the excitement of the day by taking photos and videos. Share these visuals on your social media channels in real-time to engage with your online audience. Encourage attendees to take their own photos and tag your business, creating user-generated content that extends your reach.

Provide special incentives for attendees. This could include exclusive discounts, free samples, or branded merchandise. Collect contact information from visitors through a raffle or sign-up form for future marketing efforts.

Monitor the flow of customers and address any issues promptly. Ensure that your point-of-sale systems are functioning smoothly and that inventory levels are sufficient to meet demand. Be prepared to handle any unexpected challenges, such as long lines or technical glitches, quickly and efficiently.

Engage with customers throughout the day. Take the time to talk to visitors, answer their questions, and gather their feedback. Building personal connections can foster loyalty and encourage repeat business.

Follow up with attendees after the launch. Send thank-you emails to those who provided their contact information, and encourage them to leave reviews or share their experiences on social media. Use this feedback to refine your operations and improve future customer experiences.

By executing your marketing and promotional activities effectively and planning engaging launch day events, you can create a memorable and successful launch. This will not only attract customers and generate sales but also establish a strong foundation for your business's reputation and growth.

Post-Launch Activities

The excitement of launch day marks just the beginning of your journey. To build on the initial momentum and ensure continued growth, it's essential to engage in post-launch activities. Gathering customer feedback and evaluating your initial performance are crucial steps in refining your operations and setting your business up for long-term success.

Gathering Customer Feedback

Customer feedback is invaluable for understanding how well your launch was received and identifying areas for improvement. Here's how to effectively gather and utilize feedback:

First, reach out to customers who visited or made a purchase during the launch. Use email surveys, follow-up calls, or in-person conversations to solicit their opinions. Ask specific questions about their experience, such as the quality of your products or services, the helpfulness of your staff, and the overall atmosphere of your business.

Encourage customers to leave reviews on your website, social media pages, and popular review platforms like Google and Yelp. Positive reviews can enhance your online reputation and attract new customers, while constructive criticism provides insights for improvement.

Implement feedback collection tools on your website and in your store. Suggestion boxes, online feedback forms, and interactive surveys can make it easy for customers to share their thoughts. Offer incentives, such as discounts or entry into a prize draw, to encourage participation.

Analyze the feedback to identify common themes and recurring issues. Look for patterns that indicate specific strengths and weaknesses in your operations. Use this information to make informed decisions about changes and improvements.

Respond to customer feedback promptly and professionally. Thank customers for their input, address their concerns, and inform them of any actions you plan to take based on their suggestions. This responsiveness demonstrates your commitment to customer satisfaction and can build loyalty.

Evaluating Initial Performance

Assessing your business's initial performance after the launch is crucial for understanding how well your strategies worked and where adjustments are needed. Here are the steps to evaluate your performance effectively:

Review your sales data to determine how well you met your launch goals. Compare actual sales figures against your projections and identify any significant variances. Analyze which products or services performed best and which ones fell short of expectations.

Monitor your marketing metrics to evaluate the effectiveness of your promotional activities. Look at website traffic, social media engagement, email open rates, and conversion rates. Determine which channels and campaigns drove the most traffic and sales, and which ones need improvement.

Assess customer acquisition and retention rates. Track how many new customers you attracted during the launch and how many returned for repeat purchases. High retention rates indicate strong customer satisfaction, while low rates may signal areas where your customer experience needs enhancement.

Examine operational efficiency by reviewing key performance indicators (KPIs) such as order fulfillment times, inventory turnover, and staff productivity. Identify any bottlenecks or inefficiencies that impacted your launch and develop strategies to address them.

Conduct a financial review to assess your overall financial health. Compare your revenues and expenses to your budget and evaluate your cash flow. Ensure that your business is on track to achieve profitability and sustainability.

Gather feedback from your team to understand their perspective on the launch. Hold a debrief meeting to discuss what went well and what challenges were encountered. Use their insights to refine your processes and improve team collaboration.

Document your findings and create an action plan to address any issues and capitalize on successes. Set specific, measurable goals for the next phase of your business and outline the steps needed to achieve them. Regularly review and update your plan to stay on track.

By gathering customer feedback and evaluating your initial performance, you can gain valuable insights into how your business is perceived and how effectively it operates. This information is crucial for making data-driven decisions that enhance your customer experience, improve your operations, and drive growth. With these post-launch activities, you can build on your initial success and pave the way for long-term achievements.

9 GROWING YOUR BUSINESS

Once your business is up and running, the next focus should be on growth. Scaling up your business involves expanding your operations, increasing revenue, and enhancing your market presence. This chapter explores strategies for business growth and expanding your product lines or services.

Scaling Up

Strategies for Business Growth
Growth strategies vary depending on your industry, market conditions, and business goals. Here are some effective approaches to consider:
Market Penetration involves increasing your market share within existing markets. This can be achieved through competitive pricing, marketing campaigns, and improving your product or service to attract more customers. Enhancing customer loyalty and encouraging repeat business through loyalty programs and excellent customer service can also drive growth.
Market Development focuses on entering new markets with your existing products or services. This could mean expanding geographically to new regions or targeting different customer segments. Conduct thorough market research to identify potential markets and tailor your approach to meet the specific needs and preferences of these new customers.
Product Development entails creating new products or services to cater to your existing market. Innovation is key here, whether by improving current offerings, adding complementary products, or developing entirely new solutions. Investing in research and development and gathering customer feedback can guide your product development efforts.
Diversification involves entering entirely new markets with new products or services. This strategy can spread risk and open up new revenue streams. However, it requires careful planning and market research to ensure that the new venture aligns with your business capabilities and market demand.
Partnerships and Alliances can facilitate growth by leveraging the strengths of other businesses. Strategic partnerships, joint ventures, or alliances with

complementary businesses can enhance your market reach, share resources, and introduce new capabilities. Collaborations can also help in sharing risks and costs associated with growth.

Expanding Product Lines or Services

Expanding your product lines or services is a natural progression for growing your business. Here's how to approach this expansion effectively:

Begin with market research to identify opportunities for new products or services. Understand the needs and preferences of your current customers and potential markets. Analyze trends, competitor offerings, and gaps in the market to pinpoint areas where you can introduce new offerings.

Engage with your customers to gather feedback and ideas for new products or services. Surveys, focus groups, and direct conversations can provide valuable insights into what your customers want and need. Customer feedback ensures that your new offerings will be well-received and relevant.

Evaluate the feasibility of new product or service ideas. Consider factors such as production costs, required resources, and potential profitability. Conduct a SWOT analysis (Strengths, Weaknesses, Opportunities, Threats) to assess the risks and benefits associated with each idea.

Develop prototypes or pilot versions of new products or services. This allows you to test them in the market and gather feedback before a full-scale launch. Use the pilot phase to refine your offerings based on customer responses and operational learnings.

Plan your marketing strategy for the new products or services. Clearly communicate the benefits and features to your target audience. Use a mix of marketing channels, such as social media, email campaigns, and in-store promotions, to generate awareness and drive sales.

Ensure your operations can support the expanded offerings. This includes securing reliable suppliers, increasing production capacity, and training your staff. Efficient operations are crucial to delivering new products or services without compromising quality or customer satisfaction.

Monitor the performance of new products or services closely. Track sales, customer feedback, and market trends to assess their success. Be prepared to make adjustments based on performance data and customer input. Continuous improvement is key to sustaining growth.

By employing effective growth strategies and expanding your product lines or services, you can scale up your business and increase your market presence. This proactive approach to growth ensures that your business remains competitive, meets evolving customer needs, and continues to thrive in a dynamic market environment.

Customer Retention

As your business grows, retaining existing customers becomes just as important as acquiring new ones. Customer retention not only ensures a steady revenue stream but also enhances your brand's reputation and loyalty. This section will focus on the importance of customer service and building customer loyalty programs to keep your customers coming back.

Importance of Customer Service

Exceptional customer service is a cornerstone of successful customer retention. It involves more than just resolving issues; it's about creating positive experiences that make customers feel valued and appreciated.

Providing excellent customer service starts with understanding your customers' needs and expectations. Train your staff to be attentive, empathetic, and responsive. Ensure they have the knowledge and tools necessary to assist customers effectively and efficiently.

Make it easy for customers to contact you. Offer multiple channels of communication, such as phone, email, live chat, and social media. Respond promptly to inquiries and resolve issues as quickly as possible. A swift, effective response can turn a negative experience into a positive one, enhancing customer satisfaction.

Personalize your interactions with customers. Use customer data to tailor your communications and offers. Address customers by their names and reference their past interactions or purchases. Personalized service makes customers feel recognized and valued, fostering a stronger connection to your brand.

Solicit feedback regularly to understand how well you are meeting your customers' needs. Use surveys, feedback forms, and direct conversations to gather insights. Act on this feedback to improve your products, services, and customer service practices. Showing customers that you value their input and are committed to improvement can significantly enhance loyalty.

Building Customer Loyalty Programs

Customer loyalty programs are an effective way to reward repeat customers and encourage ongoing engagement with your brand. These programs can take various forms, but their goal is to provide value that keeps customers coming back.

Start by designing a loyalty program that aligns with your business model and customer preferences. Common types of programs include points-based systems, where customers earn points for purchases that can be redeemed for discounts or rewards, and tiered programs, where customers unlock higher levels of benefits as they spend more.

Ensure the rewards are attractive and relevant to your customers. Offer discounts, exclusive products, early access to sales, or special services that enhance their experience. The rewards should be achievable and provide tangible value to incentivize participation.

Promote your loyalty program effectively. Use your marketing channels to inform customers about the benefits of joining. Highlight the value they can gain and provide clear instructions on how to participate. In-store signage, email campaigns, and social media posts can all help drive awareness and enrollment.

Monitor and analyze the performance of your loyalty program. Track metrics such as enrollment rates, repeat purchase rates, and customer feedback. Use this data to refine and improve the program. Regularly introduce new rewards or exclusive offers to keep the program fresh and exciting.

Engage with your loyalty program members regularly. Send personalized messages and offers based on their purchase history and preferences. Celebrate milestones such as birthdays or membership anniversaries with special rewards or discounts. This ongoing engagement keeps your brand top of mind and reinforces the value of the loyalty program.

Leverage technology to manage and enhance your loyalty program. Use CRM systems to track customer interactions and preferences. Loyalty program software can automate point tracking, reward redemption, and personalized communications, making it easier to manage the program and provide a seamless experience for your customers.

By focusing on exceptional customer service and building effective customer loyalty programs, you can significantly improve customer retention. Loyal customers are not only more likely to make repeat purchases, but they can also become advocates for your brand, driving word-of-mouth referrals and contributing to your business's long-term success.

Networking and Partnerships

Building strong business relationships and exploring strategic partnerships can significantly contribute to the growth and success of your business. Networking and collaborations open up opportunities for new markets, shared resources, and enhanced innovation. This section will guide you through the importance of building business relationships and how to explore partnerships and collaborations effectively.

Building Business Relationships

Establishing and maintaining strong business relationships is essential for long-term success. These relationships can lead to valuable opportunities, insights, and support that can help your business thrive.

Start by attending industry events, conferences, and trade shows to meet potential partners, customers, and influencers. Participate in networking sessions and engage in conversations to build connections. Be genuinely interested in learning about other businesses and how you can mutually benefit from a relationship.

Join professional associations and local business groups. These organizations provide a platform to meet like-minded professionals, share knowledge, and collaborate on initiatives. Regularly attending meetings and participating in activities can help you establish a presence in your business community.

Leverage social media and online platforms to network with professionals in your industry. LinkedIn, for example, is an excellent tool for connecting with potential partners, customers, and mentors. Join relevant groups, participate in discussions, and share valuable content to build your online presence and credibility.

Cultivate relationships by offering value first. Provide assistance, share expertise, or connect people within your network who can benefit from each other. Building a reputation as a helpful and resourceful professional can lead to more meaningful and long-lasting relationships.

Maintain and nurture your relationships by keeping in touch regularly. Send follow-up emails after meetings, congratulate contacts on their achievements, and offer to meet for coffee or lunch to catch up. Showing that you value and appreciate your connections can strengthen your relationships over time.

Exploring Partnerships and Collaborations

Strategic partnerships and collaborations can provide access to new resources, markets, and expertise that can drive your business growth. Here's how to explore and establish effective partnerships:

Identify potential partners who share your values, goals, and target audience. Look for businesses that complement your products or services, have a strong reputation, and possess resources or expertise that can benefit your business. Research potential partners thoroughly to ensure they are a good fit.

Initiate contact and propose a meeting to discuss potential collaboration. Clearly articulate the benefits of a partnership and how it can be mutually beneficial. Be open to listening to their needs and objectives, and explore ways to align your goals.

Define the scope and terms of the partnership. Clearly outline each party's roles, responsibilities, and expectations. Establish measurable goals and metrics to evaluate the success of the collaboration. Ensure that the terms are fair and beneficial for both parties.

Formalize the partnership with a written agreement. This agreement should include all the details of the collaboration, including the scope of work, timelines, financial arrangements, confidentiality clauses, and any other relevant terms. Having a formal agreement helps prevent misunderstandings and provides a clear framework for the partnership.

Communicate regularly with your partners to ensure the collaboration is progressing smoothly. Schedule regular check-ins to discuss progress, address any challenges, and make necessary adjustments. Open and transparent communication is key to maintaining a successful partnership.

Evaluate the outcomes of the partnership periodically. Assess whether the collaboration is meeting its goals and delivering the expected benefits. Gather feedback from all involved parties and use this information to improve future partnerships.

Be open to exploring different types of collaborations. Partnerships can take various forms, such as joint ventures, co-marketing campaigns, product development collaborations, or shared resources agreements. Being flexible and creative in your approach can lead to innovative and impactful collaborations.

By building strong business relationships and exploring strategic partnerships, you can expand your network, access new opportunities, and drive your business growth. Networking and collaborations not only enhance your business capabilities but also create a supportive ecosystem that fosters innovation and success.

10 STAYING RESILIENT AND ADAPTIVE

Resilience and adaptability are crucial traits for long-term business success. Every business faces challenges and setbacks, and the ability to navigate these difficulties effectively can make the difference between success and failure. This chapter explores common obstacles in business and strategies for overcoming them, ensuring that you stay resilient and adaptive in the face of adversity.

Handling Challenges and Setbacks

Common Obstacles in Business

Every business encounters a variety of challenges that test its resilience. Some of the most common obstacles include:

Financial difficulties often arise due to cash flow problems, unexpected expenses, or insufficient funding. These issues can threaten the sustainability of your business if not addressed promptly.

Market competition is a constant challenge, requiring you to stay ahead of competitors by continuously improving your products, services, and customer experience.

Operational issues such as supply chain disruptions, equipment failures, or staff shortages can hinder your ability to deliver products or services effectively.

Regulatory changes and compliance requirements can impose additional costs and operational complexities. Staying informed and compliant with industry regulations is essential but can be challenging.

Customer dissatisfaction due to product or service issues, poor customer service, or unmet expectations can damage your reputation and impact sales.

Technological advancements can render existing processes, products, or services obsolete. Keeping up with technological changes is crucial to maintaining competitiveness.

Strategies for Overcoming Challenges

To overcome these common obstacles, it's essential to develop effective strategies that enhance your resilience and adaptability:

Maintain a healthy cash flow by regularly monitoring your finances, forecasting future needs, and planning for contingencies. Create a cash reserve to cover unexpected expenses and ensure you have access to credit if needed.

Conduct regular market research to stay informed about industry trends, customer preferences, and competitor activities. Use this information to adjust your strategies, innovate, and differentiate your offerings.

Develop robust operational processes and contingency plans. Identify potential risks in your supply chain, equipment, and workforce, and create backup plans to mitigate these risks. Regularly review and update these plans to ensure they remain effective.

Stay informed about regulatory changes that affect your industry. Join industry associations, subscribe to relevant publications, and consult with legal experts to ensure compliance. Proactively adapting to new regulations can prevent costly penalties and disruptions.

Prioritize customer satisfaction by focusing on delivering high-quality products and services and providing excellent customer support. Regularly seek customer feedback and use it to make improvements. Address customer complaints promptly and effectively to maintain trust and loyalty.

Embrace technological advancements by investing in new technologies that improve efficiency, productivity, and customer experience. Stay current with industry innovations and consider how they can benefit your business. Training your team to adapt to new technologies is also crucial.

Cultivate a resilient mindset within your team. Encourage a culture of continuous learning, flexibility, and problem-solving. Support your employees through training and development programs that enhance their skills and adaptability.

Build a strong support network of mentors, advisors, and peers. Surrounding yourself with experienced and knowledgeable individuals can provide valuable insights, guidance, and encouragement when facing challenges.

Communicate transparently with your team about challenges and setbacks. Keeping your employees informed and involved in problem-solving fosters a collaborative environment and boosts morale.

Learn from failures and setbacks. Analyze what went wrong, identify the root causes, and implement changes to prevent similar issues in the future. Viewing setbacks as learning opportunities rather than failures can strengthen your resilience.

By understanding common obstacles in business and developing strategies to overcome them, you can enhance your resilience and adaptability. These qualities are essential for navigating the uncertainties and challenges that come with running a business. Staying resilient and adaptive ensures that you can continue to grow, innovate, and succeed, no matter what challenges you face.

Adapting to Change

In the ever-evolving business landscape, the ability to adapt to change is crucial for long-term success. Flexibility and staying updated with industry trends enable businesses to remain competitive and responsive to market demands. This section will explore the importance of flexibility and how to stay informed about industry trends.

Importance of Flexibility

Flexibility is a key trait for any successful business. It allows you to respond quickly to changes in the market, customer preferences, and external conditions. Here are some reasons why flexibility is essential:

Flexibility enables you to pivot your business strategy when necessary. Whether it's adjusting your product line, changing your marketing approach, or exploring new revenue streams, being adaptable helps you navigate through uncertainties and seize new opportunities.

It improves your ability to manage risks. By anticipating potential changes and preparing to adapt, you can mitigate the impact of unforeseen events, such as economic downturns, supply chain disruptions, or technological shifts.

Flexibility fosters innovation. Encouraging a flexible mindset within your team promotes creative thinking and problem-solving. It allows employees to experiment with new ideas and approaches, leading to continuous improvement and innovation.

It enhances customer satisfaction. By staying attuned to customer needs and preferences, you can quickly adjust your offerings and services to meet their expectations. This responsiveness builds customer loyalty and trust.

Staying Updated with Industry Trends

Staying informed about industry trends is critical for making strategic decisions and maintaining a competitive edge. Here are some strategies to keep up-to-date with the latest developments in your industry:

Regularly read industry publications, blogs, and news sites. Subscribing to relevant magazines, journals, and online platforms ensures you receive the latest information on market trends, technological advancements, and regulatory changes.

Join industry associations and professional organizations. These groups often provide valuable resources, such as newsletters, webinars, and conferences, where you can learn about the latest trends and network with other professionals.

Attend industry conferences, trade shows, and workshops. These events offer opportunities to hear from industry leaders, discover new products and services, and gain insights into emerging trends. They also provide a platform for networking and building relationships with peers and potential partners.

Engage with thought leaders and influencers in your industry. Follow them on social media, read their blogs, and participate in discussions. Thought leaders often share valuable insights and perspectives on current and future trends.

Conduct market research and surveys. Regularly gathering data on your target market and competitors helps you identify shifts in customer preferences and emerging trends. Use this information to adjust your strategies and stay ahead of the competition.

Leverage technology to monitor trends. Use tools like Google Trends, social media analytics, and industry-specific software to track changes in market sentiment and consumer behavior. These tools provide real-time data that can inform your decision-making.

Encourage continuous learning within your team. Promote a culture of ongoing education and development by providing access to training programs, courses, and industry certifications. Keeping your team updated with the latest skills and knowledge ensures your business remains adaptable and innovative.

Set up alerts and notifications for industry news. Use tools like Google Alerts to receive updates on specific topics, competitors, or trends relevant to your business. This proactive approach ensures you are always informed about significant developments.

Collaborate with other businesses and institutions. Partnerships with universities, research organizations, and other businesses can provide access to cutting-edge research, technologies, and insights that can help you stay ahead of industry trends.

By prioritizing flexibility and staying updated with industry trends, your business can adapt to changes more effectively and maintain a competitive edge. Embracing change and being proactive in your approach to new developments ensures that your business remains resilient, innovative, and prepared for future challenges.

Continuous Learning and Improvement

In the rapidly changing business world, continuous learning and improvement are essential for maintaining a competitive edge and fostering a culture of innovation. Investing in both personal and professional growth ensures that you and your team are equipped with the latest knowledge and skills to drive the business forward. This section will explore the importance of investing in growth and provide resources for ongoing education and development.

Investing in Personal and Professional Growth

Continuous learning starts with a commitment to personal and professional development. Here are key reasons why investing in growth is crucial:

Personal growth enhances leadership skills. As a business leader, developing your skills in communication, decision-making, and emotional intelligence can improve your ability to lead and inspire your team effectively.

Professional development keeps your knowledge current. Regularly updating your skills and expertise ensures you stay relevant in your industry and can adapt to new challenges and opportunities.

Investing in growth boosts innovation and creativity. Learning new concepts and exploring different perspectives can spark innovative ideas and solutions that drive your business forward.

Continuous learning fosters a growth mindset. Embracing the idea that skills and intelligence can be developed through effort and perseverance encourages resilience and a proactive approach to challenges.

Professional growth enhances employee engagement and retention. Providing opportunities for development shows employees that you value their growth, which can increase job satisfaction and loyalty.

Resources for Ongoing Education and Development

There are numerous resources available to support continuous learning and improvement. Here are some valuable options to consider:

Online Courses and Certifications: Platforms like Coursera, Udemy, LinkedIn Learning, and edX offer a wide range of courses and certifications in various fields. These courses are often flexible and can be completed at your own pace, making them ideal for busy professionals.

Workshops and Seminars: Attend workshops and seminars related to your industry or areas of interest. These events provide hands-on learning experiences and opportunities to engage with experts and peers.

Professional Associations: Join professional organizations relevant to your industry. These associations often offer resources such as webinars, journals, and networking events that can enhance your knowledge and skills.

Mentorship Programs: Seek out mentors who can provide guidance, advice, and support. Mentorship relationships can offer valuable insights based on real-world experience and help you navigate your career and business challenges.

Books and Publications: Read books, journals, and articles related to your field. Staying informed through reading can expand your knowledge and keep you updated on the latest trends and best practices.

Conferences and Trade Shows: Attend industry conferences and trade shows to learn about new developments, network with professionals, and gain insights from keynote speakers and panel discussions.

Podcasts and Webinars: Listen to podcasts and watch webinars on topics relevant to your business. These resources are often free and provide convenient ways to learn from experts and industry leaders.

Company-Sponsored Training: Implement training programs within your organization. Provide access to workshops, courses, and development programs that align with your business goals and employee needs.

Peer Learning Groups: Form or join peer learning groups where you can share knowledge, discuss challenges, and learn from each other's experiences. Peer groups can provide a supportive environment for continuous growth.

Online Communities and Forums: Participate in online communities and forums related to your industry or interests. Engaging in discussions and sharing knowledge with peers can broaden your understanding and keep you connected to the latest developments.

By investing in personal and professional growth and utilizing available resources for ongoing education and development, you can ensure continuous improvement and adaptability in your business. Encouraging a culture of learning within your organization not only enhances individual skills but also drives collective success and innovation. Continuous learning and improvement are key to staying resilient and thriving in an ever-changing business environment.

CONCLUSION

As you reach the conclusion of this guide, it's important to reflect on the journey you've undertaken and the knowledge you've gained. Starting your own business is a challenging yet rewarding endeavor, and being well-prepared is crucial for success. This final chapter will summarize the main takeaways, provide encouragement to inspire action, and offer guidance on the next steps and resources for further learning and support.

Recap of Key Points

Throughout this book, we've explored the essential elements of starting and growing a business. We've covered how to identify and validate business ideas, the importance of a detailed business plan, and the steps to choosing the right legal structure. You've learned about financing options, building a strong brand, setting up efficient operations, and executing a successful launch. We've also discussed strategies for scaling up, retaining customers, and adapting to change. The emphasis on continuous learning and improvement has highlighted the need to stay informed and adaptable in a dynamic business environment.

Encouragement for New Entrepreneurs

Embarking on the entrepreneurial journey is both challenging and exhilarating. Remember that every successful entrepreneur started where you are now, with a vision and the determination to make it a reality. Embrace the challenges as opportunities to learn and grow, and don't be afraid to take risks. Your perseverance, creativity, and resilience will be the driving forces behind your success. Believe in yourself and your vision, and stay committed to your goals. The path may not always be easy, but the rewards of building something meaningful and impactful are worth the effort.

Next Steps

As you conclude this guide, consider the following next steps to continue your entrepreneurial journey:

Implement the knowledge and strategies you've gained from this book. Begin by creating or refining your business plan, validating your ideas, and taking the initial steps to set up your business.

Seek support and mentorship by connecting with experienced entrepreneurs, joining professional associations, and participating in networking events. Surrounding yourself with supportive individuals can provide valuable guidance and encouragement.

Continue learning by staying updated with industry trends, attending workshops and conferences, and investing in ongoing education and development. Continuous learning will keep you adaptable and innovative.

Monitor your business performance regularly, gather feedback, and be prepared to make adjustments. Flexibility and responsiveness are key to navigating the dynamic business landscape.

Leverage resources such as online courses, professional associations, books, and online communities. These resources can provide further learning and support as you grow your business.

Starting and growing a business is a journey filled with ups and downs, but with determination, resilience, and the right strategies, you can achieve success. This book has provided you with a comprehensive roadmap to guide you through the process. Now, it's time to take action, turn your dreams into reality, and build a business that makes a positive impact. Good luck on your entrepreneurial journey!

Thank you for reading this guide and embarking on your entrepreneurial journey with me. If you're interested in further expanding your skill set, be sure to check out my other book, "How to be a Successful Blogger."

www.ingramcontent.com/pod-product-compliance
Lightning Source LLC
Chambersburg PA
CBHW071958210526
45479CB00003B/984